THE STORY OF
SONY

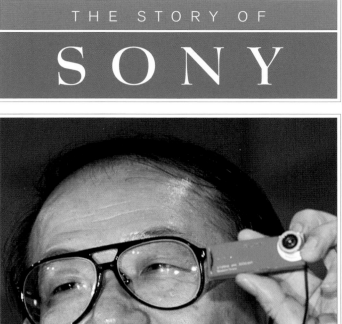

A A R O N   F R I S C H

A⁺

Published by Smart Apple Media
1980 Lookout Drive, North Mankato, Minnesota 56003

Photographs by Patrick Barta Photography, Corbis (AFP, Bettmann,
Thomas Dallal, Rufus R. Folkks, Steve Raymer, Reuters
NewMedia Inc.), Sony Corporation

Library of Congress Cataloging-in-Publication Data
Frisch, Aaron.
The story of Sony / by Aaron Frisch.
p. cm. — (Built for success)
Summary: Describes the origins and growth of the company which
began making transistor radios in Japan at the end of World War II
and has become known for the quality of its electronics products.
Includes bibliographical references.
ISBN 1-58340-296-9
1. Sonå Kabushiki Kaisha—History—Juvenile literature. 2. Electronic
industries—Japan—History—Juvenile literature.
[1. Sony Corporation—History.] I. Title. II. Series.
HD9696.A3 J33415 2003
338.7'6213'0952—dc21
2002191177

First Edition
2 4 6 8 9 7 5 3 1

THE STORY OF
SONY

Table of Contents

Made in Japan

Almost everything people in North America buy has a label saying where it was made. A product might have "Made in the USA" printed on it, or perhaps "Made in Japan." For many years following World War II, North American **consumers** saw "Made in Japan" to mean that the product was inexpensive but likely of poor quality.

World War II destroyed Japan's economy. With its military defeated and many cities bombed, the nation needed to rebuild. Most Japanese companies decided that the way to do this was to copy consumer products made in wealthy countries such as the United States. They used cheap labor and materials to make their products, then sold them at lower prices.

Just after the end of the war, in September 1945, a 38-year-old **engineer** named Masaru Ibuka—with about 20 employees and $1,600 of his personal savings—formed a company that came to be called Tokyo Tsushin Kogyo K.K., or the Tokyo Telecommunications Engineering Corporation. Another engineer, a young man named Akio Morita, soon joined the team. The new company began working literally in

the ashes of World War II. Its first headquarters was a bombed-out department store in Tokyo, Japan's capital city.

When Ibuka founded the company, he had no idea what kind of product it would manufacture. He pulled his team together and organized a brainstorming session to generate some ideas. Ibuka and his staff considered producing everything from slide rules to miniature golf equipment, but eventually they decided to make electric rice steamers. Ultimately, this idea fell through. The company was never able to make a steamer that worked properly.

Japanese engineer Masaru Ibuka founded Sony almost 60 years ago

Ibuka and Morita finally decided to build an **electronic** sound-recording machine instead. In the process, they made a decision that would have a major impact on Japan's entire manufacturing industry. They knew that products that carried a "Made in Japan" label had a bad reputation, and they wanted to change this perception. Convinced that consumers would pay a higher price for products of higher quality, Ibuka and Morita were determined to build a top-of-the-line machine. "The reconstruction of Japan depends on the development of dynamic technologies," noted Ibuka.

The engineers at the Tokyo Telecommunications Engineering Corporation had the imagination to think far ahead of their time. Electronic machines in the 1940s were very primitive. Compact disc (CD) players, personal computers, and video games had yet to be envisioned, and only a few people imagined that a machine for recording and playing back sound might one day be used all over the world. Ibuka and Morita were among these visionaries.

To build such a machine, the Tokyo Telecommunications Engineering Corporation's engineers made tape out of

Masaru Ibuka (left) and Akio Morita (right) shaped the Sony mission

narrow paper strips coated with magnetic powder and looped the tape around two large reels. The engineers created many machine **prototypes**. When the machines ran, the tape spooled from one reel to the other, and sound waves magnetized (recorded on) the tape. None of the machine designs met their expectations. But the engineers kept trying, and finally, in 1950, they had a working prototype. They produced 50 tape recorders ready for sale.

Morita and Ibuka were rightfully proud of their development, but, unfortunately, the technology was so radical that

The reel-to-reel tape recorder was Sony's first innovative product

no one wanted to buy the recorders. Consumers did not understand how a tape recorder worked—or even why someone might want one. The company began selling heating pads in order to survive until its new device caught on.

The engineers were disappointed by the poor sales of their tape recorder, but they refused to give up. They realized they were facing a unique challenge. While many companies set out to fill existing demand for a product, the Tokyo Telecommunications Engineering Corporation was trying to create a new demand where none had existed before.

To spur sales, the company's **marketing** team set out to demonstrate the tape recorder's benefits to consumers. It sold machines to Japan's supreme court by explaining to the judges that the tape machine could record everything that was said in the courtroom. The team also sold machines to schools, explaining that students could learn new languages by listening to prerecorded tapes. With these efforts, tape recorder sales slowly rose.

To America and Beyond

In the early 1950s, engineers at an American company called Bell Laboratories developed a new device called the **transistor**. This small object was used to efficiently conduct electric current from one part of a machine to another. Morita and Ibuka were intrigued by the development. At the time, it was used primarily in hearing aids, but the Japanese engineers believed it might have other uses as well. The use of transistors made hearing aids much smaller, so perhaps they would have the same effect on other electronic products.

For $25,000, Morita and Ibuka bought permission to use Bell's transistor technology. The people at Bell were surprised by their interest. Ibuka told them that his company planned to make small radios. In 1955, the Tokyo Telecommunications Engineering Corporation presented its first transistor radio, called the TR-55, to the Japanese market.

In 1957, the company introduced the world's smallest transistor radio with a built-in speaker. Small though it was, the radio wasn't quite pocket size, so the company tailored shirts with slightly larger pockets for its salespeople. The radios car-

ried a new name: Sony. One year later, the company—which had grown to include about 500 employees and was worth more than $100 million—officially changed its name to Sony.

No one had ever seen such a small radio, but most Japanese families in the 1950s could barely afford washing machines and refrigerators. Few had any interest in spending 13,800 yen—as much as the average Japanese worker's monthly salary—on a radio. Sony managed to sell a small number of transistor radios in Japan, but Morita and Ibuka realized that the big money was overseas, especially in America.

Sony's portable transistor radio revolutionized sound in the 1950s

Morita took Sony's small radio to New York City to meet with potential **retailers**. Many of them said the transistor radio was too small. One company offered to buy 100,000 units, but under one condition: it wanted to sell them under its own name. Morita refused. He wanted to make a name for Sony in the U.S. Eventually, Morita found an American retailer who wanted to buy the radios in orders of up to 30,000 units at a time. Although thrilled with the sale, Morita knew that Sony would have to work hard to meet the orders, since the company produced fewer than 10,000 radios a month.

Sony's radios went a long way toward changing American consumers' attitudes about Japanese products.

Portable radios represented Sony's first big success in the United States

Americans were fascinated by the idea of a small radio that could be taken anywhere and decided to give it a chance. Before the transistor came along, the smallest radio was a little bigger than a large shoe box and had to be plugged into an electrical outlet. Once the American public saw the high quality of Sony's portable radio, almost everyone wanted one.

Sony's transistor radio changed the way millions of people around the world listened to music. It became so popular that Sony could not make them fast enough to keep up with demand.

In the late 1950s, Sony expanded its manufacturing to include other products as well. It produced microphones and cassette-tape players that were smaller than the old reel-to-reel tape machines. It also began building televisions. In 1960, Sony's engineering team introduced the world's first transistor television. In 1968, it introduced the Trinitron television, which used new technology to produce the brightest colors and most vivid images ever seen on a screen. The Trinitron became the first product to win an Emmy award—the highest honor in the television industry.

With headquarters in New York, Sony is firmly rooted in the U.S. market

The transistor radio set Sony apart from other electronics companies, and the Trinitron television was a huge success. But it was another product—the Walkman—that made the company famous. Ibuka enjoyed listening to music but found that a tape recorder was too heavy and bulky to carry around. Ibuka and Morita came up with the idea of building a small tape player with lightweight headphones so people

Akio Morita

Akio Morita learned about business early in life. His family owned a large company that made sake (SAH-kee), a popular alcoholic beverage brewed from fermented rice. Since Akio was the eldest son, his father expected him to take over the family business one day.

But Akio had other plans. Instead of going to business school, he decided to study science. He was interested in learning how things worked. During World War II, while he was attending Osaka Imperial University, he joined the Japanese navy through a special program that allowed him to continue his research at the university. In the navy, he worked on guided weapons and night-vision gun sights. After the war, at the age of 25, he and engineer Masaru Ibuka started the business that would one day be known as Sony.

In 1960, Morita moved to New York with his wife Yoshiko and their three children. The transition wasn't easy, but soon everyone in the family learned English and made American friends. Morita felt at home in both Tokyo and New York and soon became known around the world as a leader in the electronics industry. Morita realized from the earliest days of Sony that the company could not become a worldwide leader if it stayed only in Japan. Morita saw all corners of the world as potential markets for Sony.

In 1998, when Morita turned 78 years old, the company he cofounded earned more than $51 billion and employed more than 160,000 people. He died of pneumonia on October 3, 1999. Upon Morita's death, Sony president Nobuyuki Idei said, "Having been reared by Mr. Ibuka and Mr. Morita ever since joining Sony, I always viewed Morita-san as my hero."

could carry their tape-recorded music with them wherever they went—to the office, while riding on a train, or even while exercising.

In the 1970s, Sony's engineers went to work on such a portable cassette player. Working from an old cassette recorder, they first removed the device that recorded sound and replaced it with an **amplifier**, such as that used in a radio. This meant that the device would be able to play tapes but not record sound. Next, they created a set of lightweight headphones. Sony's little portable stereo needed only a trickle of

Sony's transistor television expanded portable entertainment in 1960

17

Above, a portable Sony sound system; left, an early Walkman;
right, modern Walkman models can play CDs and digital music

battery power, and the headphones produced incredible sound—even better than Ibuka and Morita had expected.

When Sony introduced the Walkman to consumers in 1979, critics predicted that nobody would buy a tape player that could not record sound as well as play it. Morita had his own worries about the new machine. He feared that many people would find the idea of listening to their own private music while in public impolite.

The critics were quickly silenced, and all doubts erased. The Walkman became an international sensation. Most consumers didn't seem to think that listening to music in public was a breach of etiquette—quite the contrary. No matter where they were, people could crank up their music as loud as they wanted without disturbing the person next to them.

Sony had struck gold with its new music machine. By 1986, the device had become so popular that a new edition of the Oxford English Dictionary included a definition of the word "Walkman." By the mid-1990s, Sony had sold more than 150 million units, and the Walkman had spawned dozens of copycat products by other electronic companies.

A New Style of Business

In the early 1960s, Masaru Ibuka and Akio Morita realized that their company's future depended on its ability to supply world-wide retailers. In particular, Sony's future depended on sales to the United States. At the time, most Japanese companies that sold their goods in America shipped them to U.S. ports, where an American **distributor** took over and delivered the product to retailers who sold the product to consumers. Each time the product changed hands on the way from Japan to shelves in

Many of Sony's products are built using an assembly-line process

American retail stores, the price of the product went up. In the process, Japanese companies also lost control over how their products were marketed.

Morita and Ibuka decided to try a different approach to putting their products in the hands of American consumers. They wanted to keep Sony involved in every step of the sales process. To do this, they decided to set up their own network of overseas offices so that Sony employees would handle everything from manufacturing to distribution to marketing and consumer sales.

The Sony name has come to represent quality to consumers everywhere

Sony Corporation of America's offices are in downtown New York City

In February 1960, Sony opened a small office, warehouse, and retail store in New York—headquarters that would become Sony Corporation of America. The company delivered Sony products directly to the store, where knowledgeable salespeople—trained and employed by Sony—could inform consumers about Sony's products. In doing so, Sony conducted business in the United States like a U.S. company would, something no Japanese company had done before. Sony branched out into other countries as well, opening offices in France, Germany, Holland, Britain, and elsewhere.

When Sony was still young, Ibuka and Morita handled almost all aspects of the company's day-to-day business. But as the company grew in size and spread to new markets, they hired other **managers** to help lead the company's hundreds of employees. Morita felt that Sony's success depended in large part on creating a sense of loyalty among the company's employees. He believed that the best way to do this was by treating them as members of a large family.

In the 1960s, Sony placed an advertisement in a Japanese newspaper that translated to English as, "Wanted:

People capable of arguing in English." Because the company had offices and factories all over the world, it needed managers who could work effectively with—and, when necessary, argue with—people of different cultures. And from **executives** to **assembly-line workers**, Morita was determined to make sure that Sony employees everywhere were treated well. "Sony has a principle of respecting and encouraging one's ability and always tries to bring out the best in a person," Morita said. "This is a vital force of Sony."

Sony's success also stemmed from its willingness to give its engineers a large degree of independence. When he founded the company, Masaru Ibuka considered it important that engineers have the opportunity to work in an atmosphere of freedom. Sony establishes clear targets for its engineers, then turns them loose to reach those targets. Once Sony makes the commitment to go ahead with a project, it never gives up until a new idea develops into an innovative product ready for the marketplace.

Entertainment and Information

In the late 1980s, Sony became a major player in the Hollywood entertainment business. In 1988, it bought CBS Records. A year later, it purchased Columbia Pictures Entertainment, one of the biggest motion-picture companies in the world. These Sony businesses—which came to be called Sony Music Entertainment and Sony Pictures Entertainment—went on to release some of the biggest albums and movies of the next decade and a half. Sony Music released albums by

Celine Dion was one of the stars of the Sony Music label in the 1990s

Tom Cruise starred in the hit Sony Pictures movie *Jerry Maguire*

such stars as Celine Dion, Michael Jackson, and Destiny's Child, while Sony Pictures released such hit movies as *Jerry Maguire, Men in Black,* and *Spider-Man*. When *Spider-Man* was released in 2002, it shattered box-office records by making more than $675 million in less than two months.

When Sony bought CBS Records and Columbia Pictures, the company gained control over huge music and film entertainment libraries. Sony hoped that by selling **software** (such as new CDs, tapes, and videocassettes), it would entice consumers to buy its **hardware** (such as stereos, videocassette recorders (VCRs), and televisions), making Sony a one-stop shopping center for anyone with an interest in entertainment and information products.

Some people questioned Sony's move into the entertainment business. After all, Sony's reputation was based on

The Many Sides of Sony

Since starting out as a manufacturer of tape recorders and transistor radios, Sony has become a multifaceted company with an array of interests. Below are Sony's 2002 earnings by its various divisions.

Electronics:	$40 billion	Movies:	$4.8 billion
Games:	$7.5 billion	Financial services:	$3.8 billion
Music:	$4.8 billion	Other:	$1.1 billion

Source: Sony Corporation 2002 Annual Report

Sony president Kunitake Ando oversaw such movies as *Spider-Man*

its expertise in electronics. Some experts in the field felt Sony should have stayed with what it did well rather than venture into unknown territory. Others considered the move a smart one that made Sony a well-balanced company prepared for the future.

Ultimately, the move proved to be a good one. By 2002, the music and movie divisions of Sony accounted for about 17 percent of its business, with each division producing sales of almost $5 billion. By merging its hardware and software, Sony

Masaru Ibuka

During World War II, Masaru Ibuka worked at the Japan Precision Instrument Company testing new equipment for the Japanese military. "We worked so hard," Ibuka recalled, "that we literally forgot to sleep or eat." After the war, a number of his fellow engineers joined him to start Tokyo Tsushin Kogyo K.K. (Tokyo Telecommunications Engineering Corporation), the company that later became Sony.

Throughout the company's history, Ibuka maintained the highest engineering standards possible. He managed his hardworking engineers by giving them the freedom to be creative and was directly responsible for guiding the engineers who invented the Trinitron color television. The success Sony enjoys today is in part due to the management philosophy implemented by Ibuka.

Ibuka was a leader who possessed two rare qualities: patience and the willingness to listen. Sony chairman Norio Ohga remembered how Ibuka explained engineering ideas to him in the 1950s. Ohga was only a student at the time, but Ibuka showed a great deal of respect for him and his abilities. These qualities, along with great vision and years of experience, helped Ibuka make his dreams come true.

Masaru Ibuka died of a heart attack on December 19, 1997, at his home in Tokyo. He was 89 years old. Until his death, he was active as the chief advisor—along with Akio Morita—to Sony Corporation.

entered the age of **multimedia**. Multimedia combines different media and technologies, such as graphics, text, video, audio, and **animation**. For instance, a multimedia product may be an encyclopedia on CD-ROM (Read Only Memory) that combines text with animation, video, and audio to explain the topics.

In 1995, combining its expertise in software and hardware, a new Sony division called Sony Computer Entertainment launched a home video game system called the PlayStation. Sony designers were determined to make their system the best one on the market, which at the time was

The VAIO computer was one of Sony's first multimedia products

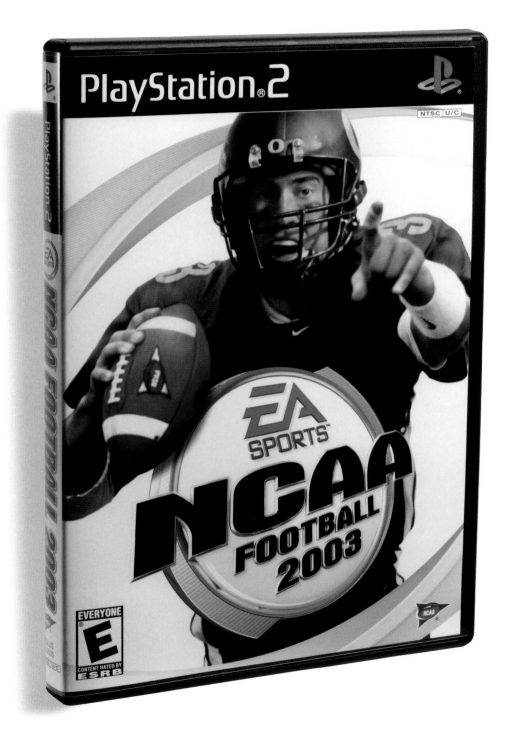

dominated by the Nintendo Corporation. One of the steps they took to do this was to replace the tape cartridges used in other systems with CDs, which could store more information. While other systems produced mostly flat, two-dimensional images, the PlayStation used advanced technology to produce realistic, three-dimensional graphics.

The PlayStation was successful beyond all expectations. Sony sold 100,000 units in North America during the PlayStation's first weekend on the market. By the end of 1996, 3.2 million PlayStations had found their way into homes throughout North America. By 1998, the PlayStation accounted for 10 percent of Sony's sales worldwide.

In 1999, Sony released the much more powerful PlayStation 2, which generated the most lifelike graphics ever seen. Consumers went wild for the system. By September 2002, 40 million units had been sold around the world, and more than 1,000 game titles had been developed. The PlayStation 2 made Sony the king of the gaming industry, out-selling rival systems such as Nintendo's GameCube and Microsoft Corporation's Xbox nearly 10 to 1.

Playstation 2 sales today make up a large percentage of Sony's earnings

A Continuing Challenge

Change happens quickly in the electronics industry. New competition and new products are constantly challenging successful companies such as Sony. Sony's electronics sales in Japan dipped in the late 1990s, mainly because other companies in the Asian market began to copy Sony's ideas and sell their lower-quality products at lower prices—much as Japanese companies had done to compete with U.S. companies in the 1950s.

Sony was faced with another problem in the 1990s. Like many companies that grow quickly with great success, Sony had begun to sacrifice efficiency and innovation for size. It rewarded its workers largely on the basis on **seniority** and loyalty—not necessarily on the basis of their ideas or contributions. Some saw Sony's size and its corporate ideal of treating employees like family as obstacles to future success.

In 1995, Nobuyuki Idei was named the new president of Sony. Idei, a Sony employee since 1960, was named to the post by the company's **board of directors**, who selected him for the job over other employees who had even more seniority. Idei made a number of changes to make the company more stream-

Portable CD/DVD players are among Sony's top-of-the-line products

SIMULATED IMAGE

SONY

lined and efficient. He reduced the company's board of directors from 38 people to 10 and brought in three outsiders to serve on the board. He also took direct control of the Sony Corporation's worldwide operations and required that all managers around the world report directly to him.

An energetic and worldly man, Idei emerged as the new face of Sony. He spoke fluently in French and English and was a marketing expert, not an engineer. Equally comfortable in Japan and the U.S., he loved to play golf and could often be seen at Hollywood parties. He also represented a new kind of

What's in a Name?

Almost all famous companies have memorable names. Akio Morita believed that the success of his company depended in part on its name. While visiting the U.S. in the 1950s, Morita noticed that a lot of companies used only letters, such as ABC, RCA, and AT&T. He thought his own company's name was difficult to remember because it had too many words. Morita wanted a shorter, more memorable name.

The name on which Morita and his partners finally settled was based on two words. As they looked through dictionaries, they came across *sonus*, a Latin word that means "sound." The company's business was recording and playing sound. At the time, Japanese frequently borrowed English slang and nicknames. The word "sonny" in English is a reference to a young son or little boy. Morita and his fellow engineers liked the name because they had always thought of themselves as bright and energetic "sonny boys."

Morita suggested that they drop one of the letters, and in 1958, the company officially changed its name to Sony. Although many Japanese at first found the name quite strange, the fact that it was rooted in English was a reflection of the global aspirations of the company's founders. The name is pronounced the same way in both Japanese and English: "SOH-nee."

business attitude in that he was willing to try new ways of doing things and to cooperate with other corporations.

Idei remained company president until 2000, when he was replaced by Kunitake Ando. During his term, Idei formed partnerships with many companies, including American companies such as Intel and Microsoft. Idei heard some criticism as he took Sony in such new directions. Many people in Japan believed he was making Sony more like a fast-moving, deal-making American company than a traditional Japanese company. But others supported the changes, confident that they would help Sony grow and remain adaptable.

Under the leadership of Idei and Ando, Sony continued to branch out into other industries in the late 1990s and early years of the 21st century. The company unveiled innovative designs in **semiconductors**, liquid crystal displays (such as those found in digital watches), DVD players, batteries, cameras, mini-disc systems (portable systems that play music digitally stored on small discs), computer monitors, flat-screen televisions, and telephones. In addition to its film studio and various record labels, Sony also operated insurance and finance businesses.

Sony is an industry leader in ultra-thin computer and television screens

In the early 1980s, Sony had made a half-hearted attempt to sell personal computers (PCs). In 1997, the company tried again. This time it launched a new PC called VAIO (Video Audio Integrated Operation). The computer had a built-in video camera for filming digital video clips and could take photographs, allowing video and photographic images to be easily transmitted as e-mail messages or combined with other multimedia content such as sound. As Sony introduced new VAIO models over the next several years, sales rose steadily, especially in Japan.

This Sony camera uses digital technology to record moving images

At the start of the 21st century, a big part of Sony's future was in **broadband** technology. This technology will enable people to communicate and access information more efficiently through the Internet and send more detailed information—including high-resolution pictures—via mobile phones and other wireless devices. People will be able to play video games with other gamers on-line. Through a new Sony service called Movielink, movie fans will be able to download and watch films on the Internet. To improve their efforts in developing such technology, Sony formed partnerships with other corporations such

Wireless Sony devices can take and send photos and browse the Internet

as AOL Time Warner (an Internet service provider) and Ericsson (a mobile communications company).

More than 50 years ago, a small group of Japanese engineers set out to develop high-quality products both useful and entertaining. By blazing their own trails, the founders of this company revolutionized Japanese industry. Having risen from the ashes of a bombed-out department store in Tokyo to become one of the world's most successful corporations, Sony continues to set the standard in electronic innovation.

Sony has risen from the vision of Masaru Ibuka half a century ago

1945   Masaru Ibuka forms the Tokyo Telecommunications Engineering Corporation.

1950   Ibuka and Akio Morita introduce Japan's first magnetic tape and a bulky tape-recording machine.

1957   The Tokyo Telecommunications Engineering Corporation builds the world's first pocket-size transistor radio.

1958   The Tokyo Telecommunications Engineering Corporation officially changes its name to Sony.

1960   Sony opens an office in New York City, creating the Sony Corporation of America.

1963   Sony unveils the world's first compact VCR.

1968   Sony wins an Emmy award for its new color television system, the Trinitron.

1969   In July, NASA takes a Sony cassette recorder on Apollo 10, the first moon-landing space mission.

1979   The public goes wild for Sony's new Walkman personal cassette player.

1982   Sony introduces its first CD player.

1988   Sony enters the music business by buying CBS Records.

1989   Sony enters the movie business by buying Columbia Pictures Entertainment.

1993   Sony starts a new computer game division called Sony Computer Entertainment.

1994   Sony introduces the wildly successful PlayStation, its first home video game system.

1998   Sony introduces the VAIO notebook computer.

1999   The PlayStation 2 is unveiled and puts Sony at the top of the video game industry.

2002   With 168,000 employees around the world, Sony earns $57 billion.

GLOSSARY

amplifier A device used to receive and transmit sound (and make sound louder) from radio waves, a tape player, or a CD player.

animation Motion pictures in which drawings or other nonphotographic images are made to move in a lifelike way to tell a story.

assembly-line workers Employees who cooperate to build a product; each worker builds one part of the product, then passes it down the assembly line to the next worker.

board of directors A group of people in charge of making big decisions for a company, such as hiring executives.

broadband Relating to technology that uses a wide range of continuous wavelengths to send information at rapid speeds; the information transfer is similar to the way that radio waves are broadcast and received by radios.

consumers People who buy and use products or services.

distributor An individual or company that sells and delivers another company's product to retail stores.

electronic Powered by an electrical current; electronic devices include televisions, stereos, and computers.

engineer A person who is skilled in the design, construction, and use of machines.

executives The leaders of a company, such as the president and top managers.

hardware Machines and the physical parts that make them work.

managers Employees who are responsible for training and supervising other workers.

G L O S S A R Y

marketing The process of advertising products in order to sell them to consumers.

multimedia The use of several technologies at the same time, such as the combination of computer software, music, and animation to create a video game.

prototypes The first working models of a new product; prototypes are usually improved and then produced in great numbers for sale.

retailers People or companies that sell products directly to consumers, usually in stores.

semiconductors Substances that conduct electricity; semiconductors are basic components used in communications equipment such as cellular telephones and computers.

seniority A ranking system based on the length of time employees have been with a company.

software The programs and systems that tell hardware how to perform tasks; examples include word-processing programs for computers or games for a video game system.

transistor A device that passes an electric current from one object to another.

INDEX

INDEX

Books

Demaria, Rusel, and Johnny L. Wilson. *High Score! The Illustrated History of Electronic Games.* New York: Osborne/McGraw-Hill, 2002.

Downer, Leslie. *Modern Industrial World: Japan.* New York: Thomson Learning, 1995.

McQuinn, Conn. *Fun with Electronics: Build 25 Amazing Electronic Projects!* Kansas City: Andrews McMeel Publishing, 1994.

Web Sites

Sony's official Web site
http://www.sony.com

Sony's official PlayStation 2 Web site
http://www.us.PlayStation.com

Sony Pictures Entertainment's official Web site
http://www.sonypictures.com

DATE DUE